Let's Find a Solution!

PBL（問題解決型学習）ではじめる総合英語

—学習者から探究者へ—

赤尾　美和　Miwa Akao
西垣　佐理　Sari Nishigaki
幸重　美津子　Mitsuko Yukishige
工藤　多恵　Tae Kudo
松田　紀子　Noriko Matsuda
板垣　静香　Shizuka Itagaki
ジョリー キム　Kym Jolley

Nan'un-do

Let's Find a Solution!

By

Miwa Akao
Sari Nishigaki
Mitsuko Yukishige
Tae Kudo
Noriko Matsuda
Shizuka Itagaki
Kym Jolley

Download Audio

音声ファイル
無料 DL
のご案内

このテキストの音声を無料で視聴（ストリーミング）・ダウンロードできます。自習用音声としてご活用ください。
以下のサイトにアクセスしてテキスト番号で検索してください。

https://nanun-do.com　テキスト番号［ **512161** ］

※ 無線 LAN（WiFi）に接続してのご利用を推奨いたします。

※ 音声ダウンロードは Zip ファイルでの提供になります。
お使いの機器によっては別途ソフトウェア（アプリケーション）の導入が必要となります。

Read by

Hannah Grace
Chris Koprowski

※ Let's Find a Solution! 音声ダウンロードページは
以下の QR コードからもご利用になれます。

はじめに

私たちは、日常生活において、大小問わず様々な問題に直面し、それらを解決しながら生きています。1人で解決できる場合もあれば、他者からの意見を参考にしたり、お互いに意見を出し合って解決することも少なくないでしょう。大学英語教育においても、知識詰め込み型から、学生自らが考え他者と協力しながら学習するアクティブラーニングを中心に進める授業が増加しています。

本書「Let's Find a Solution!」は、Problem-Based Learning（問題解決型学習）をベースに考えられた、4技能を身につける教材です。PBLサイクル（池田, *online*）と呼ばれる学習プロセスを参考に、社会・文化・健康等、身近なテーマに関する問題についての背景知識を深めます。更に解決案をグループでシェアし、最終的には短文でアウトプット（Writing, Speaking）します。段階を踏んだ学習により、無理のないグループワークへの参加を促し、学習者の自律性・思考力・発信力を鍛え、問題解決能力を育成できるよう工夫しています。

本書は全15ユニットから構成されています。各ユニットではまず**Warm up**で語彙を予習してから**Dialogue**（リスニングを含む），**Reading**へと進みます。次に、**Reading**に出現したイディオムを**Writing**問題で復習します。その後、Extension Activityとして**Dialogue**と**Reading**で学習したテーマに関する問題を解決すべく解決案を**Group Work**の中でシェアします。グループで出し合った案の中からよいと思った案を**Writing**（日本語→英語）におこし、最後に**Speaking**活動としてグループ内で発表します。Units 5,10,15では、PBLについてのColumnを読み、Word Search/Crossword Puzzleで既習ユニットの語彙の復習を行います。

コロナ禍により、対面授業から遠隔授業へと大きく授業形態の転換が迫られた中で、英語教育のあり方も更なる変革の必要性が求められるでしょう。PBLは、少人数のグループワークを中心とした学習であるため、双方向性を持つ遠隔授業（オンライン授業）においてもスムーズに取り入れることができるという利点があります。この変革の時代に、問題解決能力を身につけ、自己表現できる英語力の向上に本書が少しでも貢献できることを願っています。

なお、本書作成にあたりPBLに関する講演やワークショップを通して有益なアドバイスをくださった大阪大学の池田光穂先生、本書の企画段階であたたかい助言をくださった前南雲堂（現開文社出版）の丸小雅臣氏、編集・出版にご尽力くださった南雲堂の加藤敦氏に心より感謝申し上げます。

著者一同

参考文献：池田光穂 (*online*)「問題に基づく学習」https://bit.ly/PBLMethod

INTRODUCTION

CONTENTS
目次

CONTENTS

Unit 1 Smartphone Addiction

スマホ依存って病気だったの？

Warm up

日本語の意味を表す英語を選択肢から選んで（　　）に記号を記入しましょう。

1. 最後には（　　）
2. ゲーム障害（　　）
3. 何やってるの？（　　）
4. 中毒（　　）

5. 精神分析医（　　）
6. 精神衛生（　　）
7. 恐怖感（　　）
8. 無視する（　　）
9. 乱用（　　）
10. 見逃す（　　）

a. mental health	**b.** psychologist	**c.** What are you up to?	**d.** miss out
e. gaming disorder	**f.** ignore	**g.** fear	**h.** addiction
i. in the end	**j.** abuse		

Dialogue

次の会話を聞きましょう。その後ペアで会話を音読しましょう。

Tomo : Hi, Fumi. What are you up to?

Fumi : Not much, just checking my smartphone.

Tomo : Uh, huh. How long do you usually spend on your phone?

Fumi : Not that long really, only about 16 or 17 hours a day.

Tomo : Wow! Why do you need to be on your phone for so long?

Fumi : Well, something cool might be happening somewhere, and I don't want to miss out on anything.

Tomo : It sounds like you suffer from "FOMO."

Fumi : FOMO?

Tomo : FOMO, Fear Of Missing Out. It means you're likely to ignore other people around you because you'd rather be checking your phone.

Fumi : Yeah, that sounds like me. Also, I like playing video games on my phone more than talking with others.

Tomo : That could be a gaming disorder! I heard that half of all teenagers feel like they are addicted to their phones.

Fumi : See! I'm not the only one.

Tomo : But if you have an addiction to something, you can't stop doing it, just like alcohol and drug abuse.

Fumi : Well, I think if I went more than five minutes without my phone, I'd definitely feel nervous and probably panic in the end if I couldn't find it.

Tomo : That's not good! I read about a psychologist who said smartphones have probably led to an increase in mental health problems in teenagers.

Fumi : No kidding! Maybe my smartphone is like a drug! (220 words)

Summary

次の英文は、上記の会話を要約したものです。音声を聞いて、(　　) を埋めましょう。

Tomo and Fumi are talking about Fumi's smartphone use. When she says she spends many hours per day checking her smartphone, Tomo tells her she is suffering from "FOMO," an acronym of (1.　　　　) Of Missing Out. Although she doesn't want to (2.　　　　) on anything interesting, Tomo worries she is likely to (3.　　　　) other people because she would rather be checking her phone. He adds that a psychologist has warned smartphones have caused an increase in (4.　　　　) problems in teenagers because they can cause a kind of (5.　　　　), just like drugs and alcohol.

Reading 4 DL

次の英文を読んで、後の問いに答えましょう。

Smartphones and Mental Health

Smartphones have become such an important part of our lives that they are like an extension of our body. Some people cannot go five minutes without checking their phone. Other people might get **anxious** or panicked if they lose their phone or leave it at home. Many smartphone owners also spend a long time playing digital or video games on their phone. If this behavior becomes extreme, it may be referred to as an addiction by professionals.

"Gaming disorder" is when **repetitive** gaming behavior causes **distress** and difficulties with daily life and personal relationships. It is a mental and **behavioral** disorder that the **World Health Organization (WHO)** describes as a **clinically significant** syndrome.

However, studies show that gaming disorder only affects a small number of digital and video game players. According to a WHO expert, just as most drinkers of alcohol do not have a problem, most game players do not suffer from a disorder. It is the **excessive use** that can lead to **adverse effects** in certain **circumstances**.

Furthermore, the benefits that technology like smartphones can have on our lives must not be forgotten. Their different functions can also provide us with important information about our health. Therefore, this **versatile** device also has an **essential** role in maintaining **public health**.

(211 words)

Notes

anxious 不安な / repetitive 繰り返しの / distress 疲労 / behavioral 行動の / World Health Organization 世界保健機構 / clinically significant 臨床的に重大な / excessive use 過度の使用 / adverse effects 有害事象 / circumstances 環境 / versatile 多目的な / essential 不可欠の / public health 公衆衛生

Comprehension 1

本文から読み取れる内容を、フローチャートに日本語で記入しましょう。

1st paragraph

今や（1.　　　　）は我々の（2.　　　　）の一部になっているため、いつもそばにないと不安になる。これは一種の（3.　　　　）と呼ばれる。

2nd paragraph

WHO は、（4.　　　　　　　　）を（5.　　　　　　　　）病状と説明する。繰り返し行うことによって（6.　　　　）や体の不調をきたすことがある。

3rd paragraph

しかし、ゲームをする人の中でゲーム障害になる人は限られており、
（7.　　　　　　　　）のみが（8.　　　　　　　　）を引き起こすのだという。

4th paragraph

（9.　　　　　　　　）が我々の生活に与える恩恵を忘れてはならない。スマホは
（10.　　　　　　　　）において常に重要な役割を果たすものである。

Comprehension 2

本文の内容について、以下の質問に答えましょう。

1. Why might some people feel nervous if their smartphone is not at hand?
   a. Because they will not be able to make calls
   b. Because someone may steal it
   c. Because it helps to monitor their health
   d. Because it is like a part of their body

2. When people play video games, what can lead to gaming disorder?
   a. Substance abuse
   b. Overuse
   c. Certain applications
   d. Adverse effects

Writing

日本語に合うように、単語を並び替えて文章を完成させましょう。文頭にくる語も小文字にしてあります。

1．なぜそんなに長い間ネット検索し続けなくちゃいけないの？

Why do you (keep / the Internet / have / searching / to) for so long?

____?

2．生活態度が乱れている人は病気になりやすいらしいよ。

They say that (are / a disordered lifestyle / have / more likely to / people who) get sick.

____.

3．もし携帯電話を家に忘れてきたら、一日中落ち着かないよ。

(at home / left / if / my cell phone / I), I would be restless all day.

____.

Expressions for Problem Solving

・What about …? （～はどうですか？）

What about making it a rule not to check it for a certain length of time?

・Why don’t we …? （～しませんか？）

Why don’t we start working on positive aspects of the smartphone?

・I plan to … （私は～するつもりです）

I’m planning to solve this problem in three steps.

Extension Activity

Group Work

スマホ使い過ぎ防止の対策案をグループで出し合い、メモしましょう。

Notes

Writing

グループで出し合った案の中からいいと思ったものを３つ選んで書き出しましょう。

日本語

1. ______________________________
2. ______________________________
3. ______________________________

英語

1. ______________________________
2. ______________________________
3. ______________________________

Speaking

３つの案をグループ内で発表し合いましょう。Evaluation Form にお互いの評価を記入しましょう。

Unit 2 Congestion at the Cafeteria

学生食堂の混雑を解決したい！

Warm up

日本語の意味を表す英語を選択肢から選んで（　　）に記号を記入しましょう。

学生食堂の混雑

Crowded Cafeteria

1. かろうじて（　　）
2. 食事（　　）
3. 話し合う（　　）
4. 解決(策)（　　）
5. 把握（　　）
6. 調査（　　）
7. 同僚、仲間（　　）
8. ～に加えて（　　）
9. 行う（　　）
10. 具体的に（　　）

a. peer	b. barely	c. survey	d. conduct
e. specifically	f. meal	g. in addition to	h. discuss
i. grasp	j. solution		

Dialogue

次の会話を聞きましょう。その後ペアで会話を音読しましょう。

Tomo : Hey, you barely made it to class! What took you so long?

Fumi : Guess? As usual, the cafeteria was so crowded! First, I had to wait in the huge line to get my ticket from the machine. Then I had to wait some more for my meal.

Tomo : Sorry to hear that. I've never seen such a busy cafeteria, even back at my university in the U.S.

Fumi : I wonder why our cafeteria is so crowded every day.

Tomo : There must be a way everyone can use the cafeteria more easily.

Fumi : I have an idea! Why don't we find a solution? First, we need a better grasp of the situation.

Tomo : OK, let's take pictures of the cafeteria at different times of the day. Then we can check when the busiest hours are.

Fumi : That's a great idea! What else do you think we should do?

Tomo : How about a survey to see what our peers think about this problem?

Fumi : Good idea! In addition to the survey, why don't we conduct interviews with some students in order to learn how they specifically use the cafeteria?

Tomo : Also, there must be information on the Internet that will help us find solutions for overcrowded cafeterias.

Fumi : Great! Now, let's discuss who does what! (202 words)

Summary

次の英文は、上記の会話を要約したものです。音声を聞いて、(　　) を埋めましょう。

Tomo and Fumi are talking about how the cafeteria is always (1. 　　　　). They decide to find a (2. 　　　　). To get a better (3. 　　　　) of the situation, they decide to check when are the busiest hours. Tomo suggests a (4. 　　　　) to find out the opinions of their peers. Other ideas they discuss are (5. 　　　　) interviews and checking information on the Internet.

Reading

次の英文を読んで、後の問いに答えましょう。

Students Complain about Crowded Cafeteria

Jessica and Dan waited for nearly **half an hour** in the cafeteria line at their university today. When they finally came through the lunch line, they had only 10 minutes left to finish their lunches before their afternoon classes. Like other students, they often complain that their university should have at least one more cafeteria so that students have enough time to eat during the **relatively brief** lunch break. **On behalf of** such students, the **Student Body Association** made an **official** complaint to the university last fall.

Since then, the university and the company that **runs** the cafeteria have discussed the **issue** and ways to solve it many times. Recently, they introduced the “Cafeteria Prepaid Card” as their solution. They explained, “Whenever students make an **advance payment** on their cards for lunches, an extra 10% will be added to this prepaid amount. Also, if students start using this card, they will spend less time waiting in lines since there will be less cash **transactions**.”

However, **so far**, it does not seem to be working well. Students are still waiting in long **queues**, and the cafeteria is as crowded **as always**. When asked about this, Jessica said, “The prepaid card isn’t working because it doesn’t fix the **fundamental** problem. We need more **productive** ideas, such as **food trucks** or sandwich shops on campus, and of course, another cafeteria would be very helpful.”

(231 words)

Notes

half an hour 30分 / relatively 比較的 / brief 短い / on behalf of ～を代表して / Student Body Association 学生自治会 / official 公式な / run 経営する / issue 問題 / advance payment 前払い / transaction 取り引き、やり取り、処理 / so far 今のところ / queue 列 / as always 相変わらず / fundamental 根本的な / productive 生産的な / food truck 移動屋台

Comprehension 1

本文から読み取れる内容を、フローチャートに日本語で記入しましょう。

1st paragraph

昼休みが短いのに食堂が混雑し、ゆっくり食べる暇がないという学生の声を(1.　　　)し、(2.　　　　　)が、大学に(3.　　　　)を訴えた。

2nd paragraph

大学は、チャージする度に(4.　　)%が上乗せされるプリペイドカードを(5.　　　)した。(6.　　)のやり取りが少なくなり、列の混雑が緩和されると期待されていた。

3rd paragraph

しかし、(7.　　　　)、あまりうまくいっていないようだ。学生は、まだ長い列に並んでいるし、食堂は(8.　　　)通りに混雑している。プリペイドカードは(9.　　)解決にならないので、(10.　　　)やサンドイッチ店を大学内に用意すべきという学生の声もある。

Comprehension 2

本文の内容について、以下の質問に答えましょう。

1. Which statement is true about the congested cafeteria?
   a. Students have only 30 minutes for their lunch break.
   b. The Student Body Association introduced the idea of the prepaid card.
   c. Jessica does not think the prepaid card is the best solution.
   d. The university succeeded in reducing congestion at the cafeteria.

2. What will happen if students use the Cafeteria Prepaid Card?
   a. They will get their lunch as fast as students who pay in cash.
   b. They will get a 10% discount on lunch each time.
   c. They will get lunch for free if they pay in advance.
   d. They will get an extra ¥500 if they charge ¥5,000 to their card.

Writing

日本語に合うように、単語を並び替えて文章を完成させましょう。文頭にくる語も小文字にしてあります。

1．英語力を向上させるためには、文法をしっかり把握する必要がある。

In order to improve your English skills, you need to (good / have / of / a / grasp / grammar).

____.

2．チームを代表して、監督がスピーチを述べた。

The director made a speech (team / the / of / behalf / on).

____.

3．パン屋さんの前に、沢山の人が長い列に並んでいる。

Many people are (line / in / waiting / long / a) in front of the bakery.

____.

Expressions for Problem Solving

・Let's … （～しましょう）

Let's take pictures of the cafeteria at different times of the day.

・I recommend that … （～することをお勧めします）

I recommend that you take a survey to see what our peers think about this problem.

・Why don't you …? （～してはどうですか？）

Why don't you conduct interviews with some students in order to learn how they specifically use the cafeteria?

Extension Activity

Group Work

学生食堂の混雑を解消するためのアイデアをグループで出し合い、メモしましょう。

Notes

Writing

グループで出し合った案の中からいいと思ったものを３つ選んで書き出しましょう。

日本語
1. ______________________________
2. ______________________________
3. ______________________________

英語
1. ______________________________
2. ______________________________
3. ______________________________

Speaking

３つの案をグループ内で発表し合いましょう。Evaluation Form にお互いの評価を記入しましょう。

Unit 3 Infectious Diseases

予防は最高の薬！

Warm up

日本語の意味を表す英語を選択肢から選んで（　　）に記号を記入しましょう。

9. 感染病（　　）

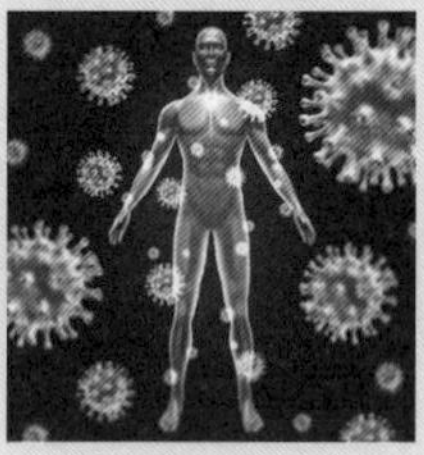

1. 悪夢（　　）
2. 習慣（　　）
3. ウイルス（　　）
4. 防ぐ（　　）
5. 無防備な（　　）
6. 濃厚接触（　　）
7. 取り除く（　　）
8. 衛生（　　）
10. 二次感染（　　）

a. nightmare	**b.** remove	**c.** virus	**d.** hygiene
e. close contact	**f.** unprotected	**g.** practice	**h.** prevent
i. infectious disease		**j.** cross-contamination	

Dialogue 8 DL

次の会話を聞きましょう。その後ペアで会話を音読しましょう。

Fumi : Hi, Tomo! How's it going?

Tomo : OK, thanks. I feel much better today.

Fumi : You mean you were sick?

Tomo : Well, I had a cold and a slight fever last week, so I canceled my part-time job to avoid close contact with others. I didn't want to make them sick too. But now I think I'm over my cold completely.

Fumi : Oh, I'm relieved to hear that. But Tomo, didn't you have a bad cold a couple of months ago too?

Tomo : Yeah, that's right. It was the flu. I suffered from that nightmare for about a week and lost 3 kilograms.

Fumi : Sounds terrible! But getting sick so often probably means you are often unprotected against infectious diseases. Maybe you need to practice better hygiene. It can help to prevent illnesses.

Tomo : Really? What do you mean?

Fumi : Well, they say that prevention is the best medicine. So do you always wash your hands before you eat something?

Tomo : No, not all the time. Does that really help to prevent sickness? Washing hands seems to be an easy way to remove viruses and germs, but I wonder if it actually works.

Fumi : Well, I'm not 100% sure. But I heard it's important to prevent cross-contamination after touching something that might have things like viruses on it. Why don't we search for some reliable information about it and other ways to keep safe from infections?

Tomo : OK, let's do it. (229 words)

■ Summary 9 DL

次の英文は、前頁の会話を要約したものです。音声を聞いて、(　　)を埋めましょう。

Tomo and Fumi are talking about Tomo's cold, from which he has just recovered. Fumi worries that he seems to be (1.　　　　　) against (2.　　　　　　　). He admits that he suffered from the flu a couple of months ago as well. Fumi knows that personal (3.　　　　　) is important when trying to avoid illnesses, so she tries to give Tomo some advice about how to (4.　　　　　) diseases. However, both of them need more information about how to protect themselves from (5.　　　　　), so they decide to research more about it.

Reading

次の英文を読んで、後の問いに答えましょう。

WHO's Recommendations to Prevent Illnesses

In order to **reduce exposure to** and transmission of various kinds of illnesses, the World Health Organization (WHO) has standard **recommendations** for the **general public** to follow. The recommendations include hand and respiratory hygiene, and safe food practices. The recommendations are as follows:

- Wash your hands with soap and running water when your hands are visibly dirty, after toilet use, and after handling animals.
- Frequently clean your hands using **alcohol-based hand rub** or soap and water in the following situations: before, during and after you prepare food, after coughing or sneezing, and when caring for the sick.
- When coughing and sneezing, cover your mouth and nose with a **flexed** elbow or tissue. Then throw any used tissue away immediately and wash your hands.
- Avoid close contact with anyone who has a fever and cough.
- If you have a fever, cough, and **difficulty breathing**, seek medical care early and share your previous travel history with your doctor.
- When visiting **live markets** in areas currently experiencing cases of **novel coronavirus**, avoid direct unprotected contact with live animals and surfaces in contact with animals.
- The **consumption** of raw or **undercooked** animal products should be avoided. Raw meat, milk, or animal organs should be **handled with care** in order to avoid cross-contamination with uncooked foods.

(211 words)

Notes

reduce 減らす / exposure to ～に身をさらすこと / recommendations 推奨事項 / general public 一般大衆 / alcohol-based hand rub アルコール入りの手の薬剤 / flexed 曲げた状態の / difficulty breathing 呼吸困難 / live market 生き物の市場 / novel coronavirus 新型コロナウィルス / consumption 食べること / undercooked 生焼けの / handled with care 取り扱いに注意して

Comprehension 1

本文から読み取れる内容を、フローチャートに日本語で記入しましょう。

自分や周囲の人々を（1.　　　）から守るには

＊（2.　　　）が汚れている時

＊（3.　　　）の後や動物を触った後

＊食事の準備の時

＊咳や（4.　　　　　）の後や（5.　　　）の世話をしている時

＊（6.　　　　　）やティッシュで口と鼻を覆う

＊ティッシュはすぐに捨てる

＊熱・咳・（7.　　　　　）がある場合は治療を受ける

＊熱や咳のある人との接触

＊動物との（8.　　　　）な接触

＊生肉・内臓等は注意して取り扱い（9.　　　　　）による（10.　　　　　）を防ぐ

Comprehension 2

本文の内容について、以下の質問に答えましょう。

1. Which instruction is NOT included in the WHO recommendations for the general public?
   a. How to clean hands
   b. How to reduce the transmission of diseases
   c. How to take cold medicine
   d. How to deal with animal products

2. What should you do if you cough or sneeze?
   a. Consume raw and undercooked meat.
   b. Cover your mouth and nose with your hands.
   c. Wash your face and hands after your meal.
   d. Throw your used tissue away immediately and wash your hands.

Writing

日本語に合うように、単語を並び替えて文章を完成させましょう。文頭にくる語も小文字にしてあります。

1. 彼はかれこれ 10 年以上も糖尿病に苦しめられている。

   He (for / diabetes / more than / suffered / has / from) ten years.

   ____?

2. マスクをすることはインフルエンザから自分を守る最も簡単な方法だと思われる。

   (the easiest way / wearing a mask / be / protect yourself / to / seems to) from the flu.

   ____.

3. その症状を癒すための昔の治療法を調べてみない？

   Why don't we (remedies / to / those symptoms / some old / look into / heal)?

   ____?

Expressions for Problem Solving

- be going to explain how to ... （～の方法を説明します）

  We're going to explain how to solve this problem. First, ...

- One of the best solutions to ... （～の最善の解決法の一つは）

  One of the best solutions to the problem is as follows.

- work out the key to ... （～の糸口を見つける）

  We worked out the key to settling the whole issue.

Extension Activity

Group Work

風邪などの感染病対策をグループで出し合い、メモしましょう。

Notes

Unit 3

Writing

グループで出し合った案の中からいいと思ったものを３つ選んで書き出しましょう。

日本語

1. __________
2. __________
3. __________

英語

1. __________
2. __________
3. __________

Speaking

３つの案をグループ内で発表し合いましょう。Evaluation Form にお互いの評価を記入しましょう。

Unit 4 Universal Design

ユニバーサルデザインって何？

Warm up

日本語の意味を表す英語を選択肢から選んで（　　）に記号を記入しましょう。

ユニバーサルデザイン
（　　　）

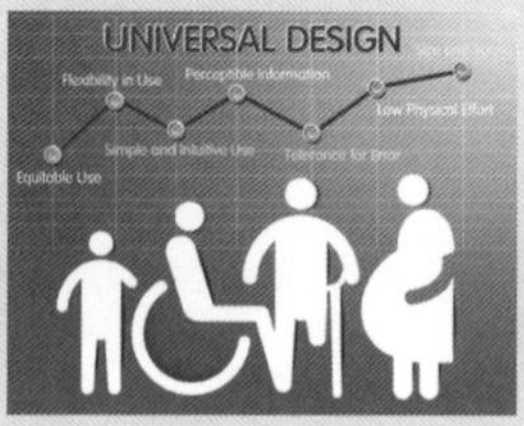

1. 書体（　　）
2. ～を表す（　　）
3. 利用する（　　）
4. ～に関わらず（　　）
5. 性別（　　）
6. 製品（　　）
7. 読み誤る（　　）
8. 自動の（　　）
9. 点字（　　）
10. 文字（　　）

a. font	**b.** braille	**c.** stand for	**d.** regardless of
e. gender	**f.** automatic	**g.** access	**h.** misread
i. product	**j.** character		

Dialogue 11 DL

次の会話を聞きましょう。その後ペアで会話を音読しましょう。

UD FONT by MORISAWA

Tomo : Hi, Fumi! What's that on the back of your textbook?

Fumi : Hi, Tomo. It's the logo for "UD font."

Tomo : What is "UD"?

Fumi : UD stands for Universal Design, which are things designed so they can be accessed and used by all people regardless of their age, gender, size, ability, etc. In short, universally designed products can be used easily by everyone.

Tomo : What a nice idea! So what is UD font?

Fumi : Well, this textbook uses the UD font. The UD font is designed to be easier to read and less likely to be misread by people than other fonts.

Tomo : Wonderful! Are there any other products that are universally designed?

Fumi : Of course! I'm sure you use automatic doors almost every day.

Tomo : Wow, I must have used a lot of UD products without realizing it.

Fumi : From now on, you will notice UD products all around you. Anyway, is there anything that you think needs to be universally designed on campus?

Tomo : Well, one of my classmates says she wishes our cafeteria menu was in braille as well. Is there anything we can do about that?

Fumi : Let's see... Why don't we go ask the Student Support Services Center? Another idea is that we can make menus ourselves by printing them in both UD font and braille! (209 words)

Summary 12 DL

次の英文は、上記の会話を要約したものです。音声を聞いて、(　　) を埋めましょう。

Fumi is telling Tomo that UD (1.　　　　　　) Universal Design. Universally designed products are useful for everyone (2.　　　　　　) their age, size, ability or (3.　　　　　　). Tomo is surprised to know that many things are universally designed, such as (4.　　　　　　) doors. Tomo and Fumi might make cafeteria menus printed in both UD font and (5.　　　　　　).

Reading

次の英文を読んで、後の問いに答えましょう。

Non-Slippery Noodles

"*Suberan Udon*" (non-slippery noodles) is a product based on the Universal Design concept. It is also the first universally designed food with a patented manufacturing method.

There are multiple slits in the center of each noodle, which open up when the udon is boiled. This makes it easy for people to pick up the noodles with a fork or chopsticks. Moreover, the soup stock soaks into the slits, so people can enjoy the flavor of the soup to the fullest.

The noodles are 18 centimeters long, which is about 10 centimeters shorter than regular udon noodles. This makes them easier to eat for people with disabilities, the elderly, children, and even people who are not familiar with using chopsticks.

Michinobu Oka, who developed the product, says that he made *Suberan Udon* with the idea of making udon easy for everyone to eat. However, during the development process, there was some criticism that the noodles were difficult to eat or cut easily. Nevertheless, he continued with his efforts.

As a result, his udon won several awards, such as the "Kobe Universal Design Award" in 2005, and the "Kids Design Award" in 2009. He hopes that he can share his happiness with the people who eat his udon.

(207 words)

Notes

slippery 滑りやすい / based on ～に基づいて / patented 特許権を有する / manufacturing method 製造方法 / multiple 複数の / slit 切れ目、切り込み / boil 湯がく、沸かす / soup stock だし汁 / soak into ～に染み込む / flavor 味わい / to the fullest 最大限に / the elderly 高齢者 / criticism 批判 / nevertheless それにも関わらず / award 賞

Comprehension 1

本文から読み取れる内容を、フローチャートに日本語で記入しましょう。

1st & 2nd paragraphs

「すべらんうどん」は、(1.   ) 食品である。麺に (2.   ) の切れ目が入っており、フォークや箸がひっかかりやすい。しかも、切れ目に (3.   ) が絡みやすく、旨味を (4.   ) に楽しめる。

3rd paragraph

麺の長さは 18 cmで、(5.   ) 麺より 10 cmほど短くなっているため、(6.   ) のある人、お年寄り、子供や、箸を使うのが苦手な外国人にも食べやすい。

4th paragraph

このうどんを (7.   ) した岡氏は、みんなに食べやすいうどんを作りたかったと言う。しかし、開発過程では、「食べにくい」「麺が (8.   )」などの (9.   ) もあった。

5th paragraph

開発を続けた（10.   )、「すべらんうどん」は、神戸ユニバーサルデザイン賞、キッズデザイン賞を受賞した。

Comprehension 2

本文の内容について、以下の質問に答えましょう。

1. Why is *Suberan Udon* a universally designed product?
   - a. Its manufacturing method is patented.
   - b. It is easy for everyone to eat because the noodles are shorter and have multiple slits.
   - c. Some people complain because it is hard to eat and cut easily.
   - d. Michinobu Oka expects people who eat his udon to feel as happy as he does.
2. Which statement is true about udon?
   - a. *Suberan Udon* is easy to eat with a fork but not with chopsticks.
   - b. Regular udon noodles are about 28 centimeters long.
   - c. Everyone has always been happy with *Suberan Udon*.
   - d. *Suberan Udon* is designed for everyone and can be manufactured by anyone.

Writing

日本語に合うように、単語を並び替えて文章を完成させましょう。文頭にくる語も小文字にしてあります。

1. バランスの良い食事を取ると、病気にかかりにくい。

   If you eat a well-balanced diet, you (sick / to / likely / less / get / are).

   ____.

2. 私の叔父は、歴史的史実に基づいた本を読むのが好きです。

   My uncle likes to read (are / that / books / facts / on / historical / based).

   ____.

3. 私のモットーは、毎日を最大限に生きることです。

   My motto is (day / each / live / fullest / the / to / to).

   ____.

Expressions for Problem Solving

解決案、提案、質問などに対するあいづち例

・What a nice idea! （それは良い考えね！）

How about a bouquet of flowers for her birthday present?
<u>**What a nice idea!**</u> She will be delighted.

・Well, （ええと、）

Which solution do you think works better?
<u>**Well,**</u> in my opinion, Plan A sounds better.

・Of course. （もちろんです）

Do you mind taking the minutes for today’s meeting?
<u>**Of course,**</u> I’ll do that.

Extension Activity

Group Work

ユニバーサルデザインにした方が良いものをグループで出し合い、メモしましょう。

Notes

Writing

グループで出し合った案の中からいいと思ったものを３つ選んで書き出しましょう。

日本語

1. ______________________________
2. ______________________________
3. ______________________________

英語

1. ______________________________
2. ______________________________
3. ______________________________

Speaking

３つの案をグループ内で発表し合いましょう。Evaluation Form にお互いの評価を記入しましょう。

Unit 5

Column 1

Problem Solving and Language Learning

14 DL

As a language learner, you are problem solving all the time. It might happen when you need to reach a certain score on a test, or when you want to communicate information but cannot **recall** important vocabulary. When these challenges occur, you need to consider different solutions to reach your goal. Your friends can be helpful too. They might offer different suggestions about the best thing to do. Sharing ideas can often lead to a better solution. In this textbook, you also work with others to consider solutions to real-life problems while you build your language skills.

This kind of practical use with others during language learning is important. It gives you the chance to use and practice the language you have learned **previously** and in this textbook. Using language is a very important step to **strengthening** your skills and **confidence**. Furthermore, collaborating with other learners gives you the chance to experience a variety of ways of expressing ideas and using language.

Working with others also gives you the opportunity to hear new **perspectives** from your group members. This may build upon your own personal knowledge of an issue or help make your own opinions clearer about a topic. Therefore, learning through problem-based activities is a great chance to build and practice your language skills while also gaining knowledge and **insights** to the world around you.

Notes

recall 思い出す / previously 以前に / strengthen 向上させる / confidence 自信 / perspective 視点 / insight 洞察・見識

Comprehension

本文から読み取れる内容を、フローチャートに日本語で記入しましょう。

1st paragraph

語学学習者としての問題の例：

・テストで一定の（1.　　　　　　）を取る必要があるとき

・情報を伝えたいのに（2.　　　　　　）が思い出せないとき

→（3.　　　　　　）が助けとなる可能性

→考えを共有することが（4.　　　　　　）とつながる

2nd & 3rd paragraphs

語学学習で大切なこと

・言語を実践的に（5.　　　　　　）こと

・他の学習者と（6.　　　　　　）こと

→（7.　　　　　　）のアクティビティ＝自分の周りの世界に対する（8.　　　　　　）が得られる

Think about Column 1, "Problem Solving and Language Learning." What problems have you experienced when language learning or communicating in English (including in this textbook)? What are some solutions you used OR could have used?

Problems

Solutions

Word Search (Units 1-4)

Find the words in the puzzle. Words can go in any direction.
Words can share a letter as they cross over each other.

Y	R	O	K	U	G	T	T	W	N	K	F	M	M	R
O	J	I	O	E	C	Y	N	U	O	E	Y	S	U	K
F	V	B	B	U	W	P	C	T	I	J	F	Y	L	T
H	Z	X	D	E	T	R	Y	R	T	J	Q	G	T	N
F	Y	N	Q	X	E	V	P	B	C	R	Y	J	I	A
P	O	G	L	B	K	E	V	Q	I	W	I	B	P	C
C	F	C	I	Z	L	P	L	U	D	N	U	T	L	I
Y	W	U	F	E	R	P	M	W	D	I	A	O	E	F
R	U	T	A	T	N	T	J	I	A	Q	K	C	H	I
G	A	N	F	Y	L	E	V	I	T	A	L	E	R	N
U	N	D	E	R	C	O	O	K	E	D	X	F	L	G
E	U	L	O	D	G	E	N	D	E	R	N	X	A	I
E	U	C	T	W	K	M	H	A	N	F	D	Q	V	S
F	R	L	P	E	O	M	A	P	C	U	S	P	V	V
W	B	W	N	R	Y	U	G	V	X	P	Q	A	E	Z

Words

addiction / conduct / gender / hygiene / multiple / relatively / significant / undercooked

Unit 6 Student Stress

ストレスと上手く付き合おう！

Warm up

日本語の意味を表す英語を選択肢から選んで（　　）に記号を記入しましょう。

学生のストレス
Student Stress

1. アルバイトをする（　　）
2. 中間試験（　　）
3. 実験（　　）
4. 講義（　　）
5. 活動（　　）
6. 自活する（　　）
7. ～を準備する（　　）
8. 小論文（　　）
9. 経験（　　）
10. 発散する（　　）

a. activity	**b.** work part-time	**c.** experiment	**d.** prepare for
e. experience	**f.** take care of oneself	**g.** relieve	**h.** lecture
i. essay	**j.** mid-term exam		

Dialogue

15 DL

次の会話を聞きましょう。その後ペアで会話を音読しましょう。

Alice : Hello, Bob. How are you doing?

Bob : Well, actually, I haven't been sleeping very well.

Alice : Why is that? What do you usually do each day?

Bob : Well, after lectures and club activities, I work part-time until late. Then I usually have to write a report on an experiment I did in class. At the moment, I also have to prepare for the mid-term English exam next week.

Alice : Oh, you are definitely overdoing it. Do you have to work late every night?

Bob : Well, my parents told me it was my responsibility to take care of myself once I got into college.

Alice : Yes, while you are at college, you definitely need to take on extra responsibilities. But university is mainly a time to learn, so why don't you adjust your club hours or part-time job a little?

Bob : You're right. The most important thing is to pass my classes so I can graduate.

Alice : That's right! But I don't study all the time. Actually, I tend to stay up late at night too. I like watching movies.

Bob : That's different to my situation. It's something you enjoy, right?

Alice : Yes, and it's an excellent way to relieve stress.

Bob : Exactly! (191 words)

Summary

16 DL

次の英文は、上記の会話を要約したものです。音声を聞いて、(　　) を埋めましょう。

Bob is explaining to Alice that he is not sleeping well. The reason is that after his (1.   ) and club activities he must (2.   ) until late at night. Then he has to write reports on (3.   ) as well as (4.   ) the mid-term English exam. Alice tells him to adjust his schedule to better fit his study needs. Alice also tells him that she enjoys watching movies to (5.   ) stress.

Reading

次の英文を読んで、後の問いに答えましょう。

The Main Reasons for Student Stress

Stress can be one of the biggest problems for college students while they are studying. There are several factors that can cause stress in students. One common cause is a **lack** of time. College students must complete many **assignments** during the semester, such as writing essays and doing experiments. They also need to prepare for their classes and review their work. Therefore, students need **plenty of** time to complete everything. Some students may not even have time to sleep, especially as deadlines for submitting assignments get closer.

Another cause of stress is **interpersonal relationships**. Students meet many people in their classes, at **extracurricular activities**, and working part-time jobs. It is quite stressful for them to **balance** the needs of studying and these personal relationships. In some cases, this may cause the **deterioration** of important relationships and lead to depression.

A third reason that students suffer from stress is **anxiety** about the future. At the end of their student life, students may start to feel stressed due to pressure from decisions they need to make about life after college. They may end up feeling even more stressed when they are unable to choose which **career path** they want to follow.

There are many other causes of stress that students may experience. However, it is important for students to find ways to relieve their stress in order to balance their mind and body.

(231 words)

Notes

lack 不足 / assignment 課題 / plenty of 十分な / interpersonal relationships 人間関係 / extracurricular activities 課外活動 / balance 釣り合わせる / deterioration 悪化 / anxiety 不安 / career path 進路

Comprehension 1

本文から読み取れる内容を、フローチャートに日本語で記入しましょう。

1st paragraph

・大学生にとって、(1. 　　　　　　) は学生生活の最大の問題の 1 つである。
・学生が抱えるストレスには、(2. 　　　　　　) がある。
・一般的な原因は (3. 　　　　　　) である。学生には数多くの課題やレポート執筆をする必要があり、すべての課題を適切にするための (4. 　　　　　　) が必要である。

2nd & 3rd paragraphs

・(5. 　　　　　　) は、学生が抱えるストレスの別の原因である。
・学生たちは学生時代に様々な人と出会うが、人間関係の (6. 　　　　　　) が時として (7. 　　　　　　) を引き起こすことになる場合もある。
・第 3 の理由は (8. 　　　　　　) である。特に学生生活の最後の方で、自分の望む (9. 　　　　　　) を選べないときに (10. 　　　　　　) ことがある。

4th paragraph

・学生が経験するストレスは他にも多くの (11. 　　　　　　) がある。
・しかし、学生自身が心と身体のバランスを保つために (12. 　　　　　　) を見つけることが大切である。

Comprehension 2

本文の内容について、以下の質問に答えましょう。

1. What is a frequent cause of stress for students?
   a. Having enough time to complete essays
   b. Not having enough time to finish essays
   c. Needing to read many books to complete essays and assignments
   d. Needing to write many essays and assignments within one month

2. When do some students have anxiety?
   a. When they start to work on their assignments
   b. When they start to make friends
   c. When they are choosing their future career
   d. When they are about to relieve stress

Writing

日本語に合うように、単語を並び替えて文章を完成させましょう。文頭にくる語も小文字にしてあります。

1. 何よりも大事なことは、あなたが健康であることです。
   (are / is / most important / that / the / thing / you) healthy.

   ____.

2. これが、彼らが会社経営に成功した主な理由です。
   (the main / they / this is / why / reason / succeeded) in running a company.

   ____.

3. 台風のため、メアリーは週末を家で過ごした。
   Because of the typhoon, Mary (staying / home / ended / the weekend / up / on).

   ____.

Expressions for Problem Solving

・The most important thing is (that) …　(一番大事なことは～です)

The most important thing is (that) you finish your assignment as soon as possible.

・This is the main reason why …　(これが～である主な理由です)

This is the main reason why Tom cannot win the game.

・end up … ing　(～で終わる)

Bill ended up missing the last train the other day.

Extension Activity

Group Work

学生のストレスの原因とその解消法をグループで出し合い、メモしましょう。

Notes

Writing

グループで出し合った案の中からいいと思ったものを３つ選んで書き出しましょう。

日本語

1. ______________________________
2. ______________________________
3. ______________________________

英語

1. ______________________________
2. ______________________________
3. ______________________________

Speaking

３つの案をグループ内で発表し合いましょう。Evaluation Form にお互いの評価を記入しましょう。

Unit 7 Black *Baito*

ブラックバイトってどういうもの？

Warm up

日本語の意味を表す英語を選択肢から選んで（　　）に記号を記入しましょう。

ブラックバイト

Black *Baito*

1. 代わりをする（　　）
2. 疲れ果てた（　　）
3. 特別手当（　　）
4. 休み（　　）
5. 労働法（　　）
6. 連続して（　　）
7. やめる（　　）
8. 休む（　　）
9. 責任（　　）
10. 上司・管理者（　　）

a. extra salary	**b.** replace	**c.** days off	**d.** miss
e. exhausted	**f.** labor laws	**g.** quit	**h.** supervisor
i. responsibility	**j.** in a row		

Dialogue

次の会話を聞きましょう。その後ペアで会話を音読しましょう。

Penny: You look exhausted. Are you OK, Toshi?

Toshi : I’ve worked 12 days in a row now, and I have to work again this afternoon. I’m always at work for much longer than scheduled too! Recently, I end up working at least 10 hours a day.

Penny: What? Don’t you think it’s against labor laws to make you work longer than you agreed?

Toshi : A few part-timers have quit working there, so they need someone to fill in, especially the evening shifts.

Penny: But it’s not your job to replace staff, right? You don’t have to feel responsible to cover all the shifts.

Toshi : Actually, I believe it is part of my responsibilities as a shift manager to help cover the schedule. I get paid more than the other part-timers.

Penny: How can you be a shift manager? You’re a university student.

Toshi : Well, my supervisor told me that it would be a good challenge for me since we all need management skills in the future.

Penny: I’m not sure if I agree. You’re working too much. You should be working hard on your studies.

Toshi : Also, the extra salary helps. You know I need to pay my rent. But you’re right. I forgot to do my homework today. And I missed all of the morning classes.

Penny: You know what? You should explain your situation to your supervisor today and ask for a few days off. (226 words)

Summary

次の英文は、上記の会話を要約したものです。音声を聞いて、(　　) を埋めましょう。

Toshi has worked 12 days (1. ________) because some part-timers (2. ________) working at his part-time job. Penny thinks that it is against (3. ________) to have him work so much, and suggests that he should take some (4. ________). Toshi agrees with Penny because he is not doing well with his school work, but he thinks the (5. ________) is helpful.

Reading

次の英文を読んで、後の問いに答えましょう。

Students Suffering in Part-Time Jobs

The phrase "black *baito*" comes from another **coined term**, "black *kigyo*." It refers to companies that **ignore** labor laws and force their employees to work under terrible conditions.

According to a survey about black *baito* conducted by the **Ministry of Health, Labor and Welfare**, approximately half of the respondents have had bad experiences at work. Employees reported that they are being **taken advantage of** or **are compelled to** work part-time under conditions that are against labor laws.

The online survey was answered by 1,000 students ranging from 18 to 25 years of age. The students who participated in the survey had part-time jobs at convenience stores, supermarkets, restaurants, and bars. Of the respondents, 60.5% of them had issues with their working conditions.

The main problems reported by the students were not getting paid for preparation and cleaning time, not being provided a break, being forced to work more days than they had agreed, and not being allowed to take days off during exam periods at school.

In response to these results, the Ministry of Health, Labor and Welfare announced that they would ask the **Japan Federation of Economic Organizations** to **prioritize** study over work for students with part-time employment.

(201 words)

Notes

coined term 造語 / ignore 無視する / Ministry of Health, Labor and Welfare 厚生労働省 / take advantage of ～を利用する / be compelled to ～するように強制される / Japan Federation of Economic Organizations 日本経済団体連合会（経団連）/ prioritize 優先する

Comprehension 1

本文から読み取れる内容を、フローチャートに日本語で記入しましょう。

1st & 2nd paragraphs

・「ブラックバイト」は「(1. 　　　　　　　　)」が由来の造語

⇒労働法を無視し、社員を (2. 　　　　　　　　) 条件で労働させる会社

・厚生労働省がブラックバイトに関する (3. 　　　　　　　　) を実施

⇒ブラックバイトとは不当に利用されたり、(4. 　　　　　　　　) に反した条件での労働を強いられたりすること

⇒回答者の約 (5. 　　　　　　) が嫌な経験あり

3rd paragraph

・調査の対象者：(6. 　　　　　　　　) 歳の学生　1000 名

・アルバイト先：(7. 　　　　　　　　)・スーパー・(8. 　　　　　　　　)・バー

・結果：60.5% の学生が (9. 　　　　　　　　) に問題があったと回答

4th & 5th paragraphs

・問題点　⇒準備や掃除に対する給料がないこと

⇒ (10. 　　　　　　) が与えられないこと

⇒同意した日数よりも多く働かされること

⇒ (11. 　　　　　　　　) に休みをとれないこと

・結果、学生には (12. 　　　　　　　　　　　　) ことを経団連に依頼

Comprehension 2

本文の内容について、以下の質問に答えましょう。

1. What is NOT a problem for part-time workers?
   a. They must clean the workplace without getting paid.
   b. They do not get any breaks.
   c. They are unable to take time off for exams.
   d. They are forced to take days off.

2. What change did the results of the survey bring?
   a. Better working conditions
   b. Improved labor laws
   c. Mutual agreement to work long hours
   d. A request to the related organizations

Writing

日本語に合うように、単語を並び替えて文章を完成させましょう。文頭にくる語も小文字にしてあります。

1．来月、休みをとったほうがいいんじゃない？

Don’t you (days / off / should / take / you / think / some) next month?

____?

2．トシはいつも同意した時間よりも、長く働いている。

Toshi always (agreed / hours / longer / than / works).

____.

3．５日間連続で働かされて、疲れて果ててしまったよ。

I’ve been (five days / work / forced / in a row / to), so I’m exhausted.

____.

Expressions for Problem Solving

・Don’t you think …?（～だと思いませんか？）

Don’t you think study should come first for students?

・Actually, I believe …（実は、私は～だと考えます）

Actually, I believe it will be a good experience for me.

・I’m not sure if I agree.（賛成かどうかわかりませんね）

I understand what you mean, but **I’m not sure if I agree**.

Extension Activity

Group Work

アルバイト先がブラックバイトだったらどうすれば良いでしょうか。「辞める」以外の対策案をグループで出し合い、メモしましょう。

Notes

Writing

グループで出し合った案の中からいいと思ったものを３つ選んで書き出しましょう。

日本語

1. ______________________________
2. ______________________________
3. ______________________________

英語

1. ______________________________
2. ______________________________
3. ______________________________

Speaking

３つの案をグループ内で発表し合いましょう。Evaluation Form にお互いの評価を記入しましょう。

Unit 8 Older Drivers

大丈夫？ 高齢者ドライバー

Warm up

日本語の意味を表す英語を選択肢から選んで（　　）に記号を記入しましょう。

高齢者ドライバー
Older Drivers

1. ～することになっている（　　）
2. 道に迷う（　　）
3. 無駄に（　　）
4. 説得する（　　）
5. 免許証（　　）
6. 物忘れがひどい（　　）
7. ～に没頭する（　　）
8. 心配（　　）
9. 傷つける（　　）
10. 認知症である（　　）

a. injure	b. in vain	c. be supposed to	d. convince
e. get lost	f. have dementia	g. forgetful	h. driver's license
i. get caught up in		j. concern	

Dialogue 21 DL

次の会話を聞きましょう。その後ペアで会話を音読しましょう。

Tomo : You didn't come to the party last night.

Fumi : Yeah. I was planning on it, but...

Tomo : What happened?

Fumi : Well, my grandpa didn't return home until late at night. He left for a *pachinko* parlor by car in the morning and was supposed to return home by lunch. But he didn't.

Tomo : Didn't you call him?

Fumi : My mom did. But he had left his cellphone at home.

Tomo : I see.

Fumi : We thought that he might have gotten caught up in playing *pachinko* and lost track of the time, so we just waited in vain.

Tomo : What happened to him?

Fumi : Well, we reported him missing to the police and they ended up finding him in the next town. The police said that he was just sitting still and looking upset.

Tomo : Oh no! Did he get lost?

Fumi : Yeah. He's very forgetful these days, so we think that he could have mild dementia. We've tried to convince him to give up his driver's license, but he won't listen. We are afraid he might cause an accident and injure someone.

Tomo : I understand your concern.

Fumi : Do you have any good ideas about how we could get him to change his mind?

Tomo : Hmmm... that's a difficult question. (196 words)

Summary 22 DL

次の英文は、上記の会話を要約したものです。音声を聞いて、(　　) を埋めましょう。

Fumi explains to Tomo that her grandfather went out in his car to play *pachinko* the previous day. He (1. 　　　　　　　　) return home by lunch, but he didn't. In fact, he (2. 　　　　　　　　). Fumi asks Tomo if he has any good ideas about how to (3. 　　　　　　　　) her grandfather to give up his (4. 　　　　　　　　) because her family suspects he might have (5. 　　　　　　　　).

Reading

次の英文を読んで、後の問いに答えましょう。

(   )

When people read of another **fatality due to** an older driver the reaction is often, "Again?" This was the case when an 83-year-old female driver caused the deaths of two people in Tokyo. Indeed, a **survey** of the magazine *Shukan Shincho* showed that **headlines** in six major newspapers all **contained** the word "*mata*" (again).

As Japan's population ages, so too do its drivers. According to *Shukan Shincho*, there were 62 **fatal** traffic accidents involving drivers 80 or over in 1993, but this had **increased** to 266 by 2014—that is two every three days. With the aging population, the increase in the number of older drivers is only set to continue.

There are many risks **associated with** aging drivers, but the biggest danger is that many of them think they are OK. According to **neuropathologist** Takeshi Iwatsubo, drivers do not need to **suffer from** something **severe** like dementia to be a danger on the roads. He explains that aging drivers have slower **reflexes** and their **vision** continues to **dim** with age. **Furthermore**, accidents caused by **the unexpected are more likely to** occur in older drivers than younger ones. For example, they may hit the **accelerator** instead of the **brake** when surprised while **behind the wheel**. (207 words)

Notes

fatality（事故などによる）死 / due to ～が原因で / survey 調査 / headline 見出し / contain 含む / fatal 死に至る / increase 増加する / associated with ～に伴った / neuropathologist 神経病理学者 / suffer from ～に苦しむ / severe 深刻な / reflexes 反射神経 / vision 視力 / dim ぼやける / furthermore 更に / the unexpected 予期せぬこと / be (more) likely to ～する可能性が（より）高い / accelerator アクセル / brake ブレーキ / behind the wheel 運転中に

Comprehension 1

本文から読み取れる内容を、フローチャートに日本語で記入しましょう。

1st paragraph

83歳の女性ドライバーが東京で（1.　　　　　）を起こし、
2人の（2.　　　　　　　　　　　　）。
・人々の反応　⇒　（3.　　　　　　　　　）

2nd paragraph

・高齢化社会において（4.　　　　　　　　　　）も高齢化している。
・【週刊新潮の調査】80歳以上ドライバーによる（5.　　　　　　　　）
　－ 1993年…（6.　　　　）件　／　2014年…（7.　　　　）件

3rd paragraph

・高齢者ドライバーについて最も危険な事は
　⇒　（8.　　　　　　　　　）と思っていること
・【岩坪威教授（神経病理学者）】
　－たとえ（9.　　　　　　　）でなくても危険である。
　－年齢と共に（10.　　　　　　　）と（11.　　　　　　）が衰える。
　－若者に比べて（12.　　　　　　　）事故を起こしがち。
　例：（13　　　　　　　　　　　　　　　　　　）

Comprehension 2

本文の内容について、以下の質問に答えましょう。

1. Why is Dr. Iwatsubo worried about older drivers?

   a. They might get lost while driving.
   b. They might refuse to return their driver's license.
   c. They might cause a car accident because of dementia.
   d. They might be too confident about their driving abilities.

2. Which is the best title for the reading passage?

   a. How to Return a Driver's License
   b. How to Stay Healthy
   c. What to Do About Older Drivers?
   d. What to Do to Improve Driving Skills?

Writing

日本語に合うように、単語を並び替えて文章を完成させましょう。文頭にくる語も小文字にしてあります。

1. 私たちは週末に映画を見に行くことになっていた。

   (to / we / shopping / were / go / supposed) this weekend.

   ____.

2. Fumi と Tomo はゲームにハマっている。

   Fumi and Tomo (playing games / up / gotten / in / caught / have).

   ____.

3. 私は日本車を買った。なぜなら性能が高そうだからだ。

   I bought a Japanese car because it (perform / highly / likely / more / to / is).

   ____.

Expressions for Problem Solving

・I think … （～だと思います）

<u>I think</u> older people should return their drivers' licenses.

・I disagree with … because ～ （～なので…には反対です）

<u>I disagree with</u> your idea <u>because</u> people living in rural areas need a car.

・That's true, but … （それはその通りですが～）

<u>That's true, but</u> older people are more likely to cause car accidents.

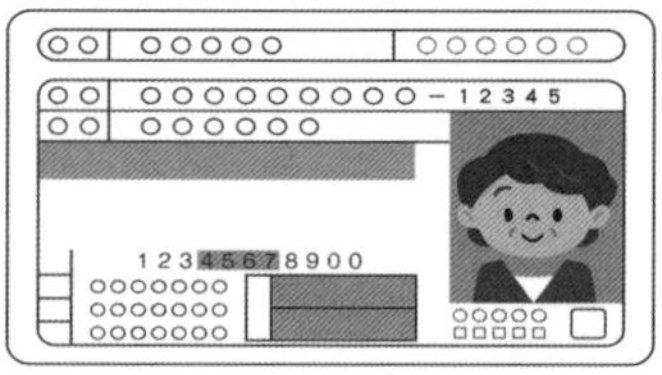

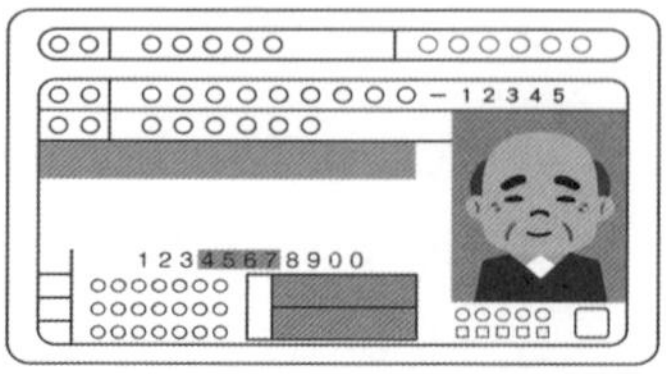

Extension Activity

Group Work

高齢者ドライバーによる交通事故対策案をグループで出し合い、メモしましょう。

Notes

Writing

グループで出し合った案の中からいいと思ったものを３つ選んで書き出しましょう。

日本語

1. ______________________________
2. ______________________________
3. ______________________________

英語

1. ______________________________
2. ______________________________
3. ______________________________

Speaking

３つの案をグループ内で発表し合いましょう。Evaluation Form にお互いの評価を記入しましょう。

Unit 9 Plastic Waste

減らそう！ プラスチックごみ

Warm up

日本語の意味を表す英語を選択肢から選んで（　　）に記号を記入しましょう。

プラスチックごみ

Plastic Waste

1. ～に立ち寄る（　　）
2. レジ（　　）
3. 大量に（　　）
4. ごみ（　　）
5. 残り物（　　）
6. (野菜の) 切りくず（　　）
7. ～の代わりに（　　）
8. 問題（　　）
9. 減らす（　　）
10. 料金を請求する（　　）

a. stop by	**b.** leftover	**c.** reduce	**d.** cashier
e. trimmings	**f.** charge	**g.** issue	**h.** garbage
i. instead of	**j.** in bulk		

Dialogue

24 DL

次の会話を聞きましょう。その後ペアで会話を音読しましょう。

Tomo : Fumi, why don't we stop by the convenience store?

Fumi : Cool! I feel like some sweets.

Tomo : Do you know what you want?

Fumi : A cream roll. I'm into Sonlaw's special cream rolls. They're really good! I'll get five so I'll have some for my family as well.

-Tomo & Fumi shop around and head to the cashier.-

Cashier : Do you need a plastic bag?

Fumi : Yes, please.

Tomo : You don't carry your own shopping bag? I usually carry some plastic bags with me instead of using a reusable shopping bag. I buy plastic bags in bulk at the 100-yen shop.

Fumi : I don't care about paying ¥3 to ¥5 per bag. Also, the small sized convenience store bags are especially useful for leftover waste like vegetable trimmings when cooking.

Tomo : You can say that again. Actually, my mom uses the larger bags she gets from the supermarket to hold the main garbage.

Fumi : Same as my mom. I think many people do that. But there are serious environmental issues connected to garbage and plastic waste. I guess that is why they want less people to use single use plastic bags.

Tomo : Yes, but I don't think charging for plastic bags helps to reduce waste.

Fumi : Maybe, but it's true that more needs to be done to protect the earth.

Tomo : Right. Why don't we discuss it over our snacks? Sugar will feed our brains. (223 words)

Summary

次の英文は、上記の会話を要約したものです。音声を聞いて、(　　)を埋めましょう。

Tomo and Fumi (1.   ) a convenience store. Fumi is asked if she needs a plastic bag by the (2.   ), and she pays for it because she does not carry plastic or reusable shopping bags. She reuses the plastic bags she pays for at the store for (3.   ) waste, such as vegetable (4.   ). As for Tomo, he usually carries plastic bags that he buys (5.   ) at 100-yen shops.

Reading

次の英文を読んで、後の問いに答えましょう。

Marine Pollution: Plastic Waste

The plastic bottles, bags, and containers that are thrown away on the street and on the beach are washed into the ocean and become **marine plastic waste**. It is estimated that the **amount** of plastic waste that **flows** into the ocean totals at least eight million tons per year worldwide. **It is predicted that** the **weight** of all marine plastic waste will be greater than the weight of all the fish in the ocean by 2050.

There have been cases where marine life, such as fish, have **swallowed** this plastic waste by mistake, thinking it was food. This can cause internal damage and **intestinal obstructions** that lead to death because the waste is **indigestible**.

In addition to the large plastic trash that **drifts** in the ocean, there are also **microplastics**, which are washed into the ocean as small **particles**. Moreover, tiny particles such as microplastics can be swallowed by fish and other sea life and **stored** in their bodies. If the fish that have swallowed microplastics are caught and sold as food, those microplastics will also be **digested** by the people who eat them.

Plastic waste not only **pollutes** the oceans, and is dangerous for **marine life**, but can also have a negative impact on the human body through the **food chain**.

(212 words)

Notes

marine plastic waste 海洋プラスチックごみ / amount 量 / flow 流れる / it is predicted that 〜ということが予測される / weight 重さ / swallow 飲み込む / intestinal obstruction 腸閉塞 / indigestible（食物が）消化できない / in addition to 〜のほかにも / drift 漂流する / microplastics マイクロプラスチック / particle 粒子 / store 蓄積する / digest 消化する / pollute 汚染する / marine life 海洋生物 / food chain 食物連鎖

Comprehension 1

本文から読み取れる内容を、フローチャートに日本語で記入しましょう。

1st paragraph

・(1.　　　　　) に流れ込むプラスチックごみの量

　⇒世界中で年間約 (2.　　　　　　　　　　　　) の試算

・【2050 年までの予測】

　(3.　　　　　　　　) の重量 ＞ (4.　　　　) の重量

2nd paragraph

・海に漂流しているプラスチックごみ

　⇒魚が (5.　　　　　　　　　　　　　　) 飲み込んだ

　⇒死に至るような (6.　　　　　　　) や (7.　　　　　　) を引き起こす可能性あり

3rd paragraph

・(8.　　　　　　　　　　　　) ☜ 細かい粒子

　⇒ 魚の体内から (9.　　　　　　　　　) に蓄積される可能性あり

4th paragraph

・プラスチックごみ

　－海を (10.　　　　　　) して (11.　　　　　　　　　　) を危険にさらす

　－ (12.　　　　　　) にも悪影響を与える ☜ (13.　　　　　　)

Comprehension 2

本文の内容について、以下の質問に答えましょう。

1. Which statement is true about microplastics?

   a. They are too small for humans to see.

   b. They can find their way into the bodies of fish and humans.

   c. They pollute the oceans, but do not damage our health.

   d. They will be reduced by 2050.

2. What can happen to fish in the ocean?

a. They have to eat so much food that they die of stomach problems.
b. They come to like eating plastic.
c. They carry a lot of plastic to the oceans.
d. They eat so much indigestible plastic that they die.

Writing

日本語に合うように、単語を並び替えて文章を完成させましょう。文頭にくる語も小文字にしてあります。

1. ショルダーバッグを買う代わりに私はリュックを買った。
I (of / a backpack / a shoulder bag / instead / buying / bought).

____.

2. この店はケーキのほかにパンも売っている。
(cakes / this shop / sells / in / to / bread / addition).

____.

3. このバンドは人気が出ることが予測される。
It (predicted / is / be / that / popular / this band / will).

____.

Expressions for Problem Solving

・It doesn't matter to me that … （～は私にはたいした問題ではありません）
It doesn't matter to me that they charge ¥3 to ¥5 per plastic bag.

・What I meant was, … （私が言いたかったのは～）
What I meant was, we should focus on reducing waste.

・Do we really have to …? （本当に～する必要がありますか？）
Do we really have to ban handing out free plastic bags?

Extension Activity

Group Work

プラスチックごみを減らすために私たちができる行動や実現可能なアイディアをグループで出し合い、メモしましょう。

Notes

Writing

グループで出し合った案の中からいいと思ったものを３つ選んで書き出しましょう。

日本語
1. ______
2. ______
3. ______

英語
1. ______
2. ______
3. ______

Speaking

３つの案をグループ内で発表し合いましょう。Evaluation Form にお互いの評価を記入しましょう。

Unit 9

Column 2

Important Points for Good Problem Solving

27 DL

All problems are unique. Even problems that seem similar have important differences. Therefore, it is essential to fully understand a problem before considering appropriate solutions. Think about the **congested** cafeteria in Unit 2. Fumi and Tomo are bothered by the **constantly** crowded cafeteria and want to find a solution. However, they do not **immediately** start discussing solutions. Their first step is to "get a better grasp of the situation." For Fumi and Tomo, this means understanding how and when the cafeteria is used. This will help them better understand the cause of the overcrowding and the times of the day it is at its worst. By researching this information, they can plan the most **effective** solution for their problem.

As with Fumi and Tomo, collaboration is often key when finding the best solution to a problem. Because we all bring our own personal knowledge and experiences to discussions, all suggestions are important. Therefore, don't be shy about speaking up and asking questions. In the same way, let your group members know if you need more time to consider your ideas. Tell them, "Just a moment, I'm thinking," if you are still planning what to say. Remember, your idea or question might just lead to the **ultimate** solution.

Notes

congested 混雑した / constantly いつも / immediately ～ただちに / effective 効果的な / ultimate 最終的な

Comprehension

本文から読み取れる内容を、フローチャートに日本語で記入しましょう。

1st paragraph

似ている問題であっても（1.　　　　　　　）がある。

（2.　　　　　　　）を検討する前に問題を十分に理解することが大切

例：Unit 2の（3.　　　　　　　）食堂

→（4.　　　　　　　）、いつ食堂が利用されているかを調査すること

2nd paragraph

問題解決のためには（5.　　　　　　　）が鍵　←みんなの（6.　　　　　　　）が重要

→恥ずかしがらずに発言や（7.　　　　　　　）をすることが大切

→自分の（8.　　　　　　　）や質問が最終的な解決策につながることも

❖ Think about Column 2, "Important Points for Good Problem Solving." Is there something that needs improving in your local area? Write about the problem and what you might need to research before talking about the best solution.

Problem

Things to research about the problem

Crossword Puzzle (Units 6-9)

Use the clues to fill in the puzzle below. Words go across or down. Letters are shared when the words intersect.

ACROSS

4. to persuade someone

5. a formal talk by a specialist given to a group of people, especially university students

7. to keep things in a special place for use in the future

8. to intentionally not listen or give attention to

DOWN

1. a person whose job is to receive and pay out money in a shop

2. needed or required

3. an uncomfortable feeling of worry

6. to have within

Unit 11 Overtourism

インバウンド旅行で観光公害？

Warm up

日本語の意味を表す英語を選択肢から選んで（　　）に記号を記入しましょう。

観光公害

overtourism

1. もう少しで（　　）
2. よくある（　　）
3. バスを逃す（　　）
4. 混雑した（　　）
5. 紅葉(の)（　　）
6. 公共の乗り物（　　）
7. 麻痺する（　　）
8. 荷物（　　）
9. 分散させる（　　）
10. 隠れ名所（　　）

a. public transportation	**b.** that happens	**c.** be crowded	**d.** be paralyzed
e. hidden beauty spot	**f.** autumn foliage	**g.** miss a bus	**h.** disperse
i. almost	**j.** luggage		

Dialogue 28 DL

次の会話を聞きましょう。その後ペアで会話を音読しましょう。

Hiro : Get this! I was almost late today!

Yuki : Really? That’s unusual. What happened?

Hiro : I set the alarm on my phone, but I forgot to charge it, so it died.

Yuki : Oh, that happens sometimes. When I started college, I was almost late a few times too.

Hiro : Oh, really? Why?

Yuki : There were a lot of tourists back then, remember? I missed a few buses because there were long lines and I couldn’t get on. It was all because of the tourists.

Hiro : Yeah, I remember. It was really crowded during the autumn foliage season, wasn’t it?

Yuki : Yeah, it was. There were so many tourists that the public transportation system became paralyzed. I’ve heard this kind of situation is called “overtourism.”

Hiro : It was definitely a tough time. There were so many people with large suitcases and luggage that the conductor said to get off from the back of the bus, since we couldn’t get to the front.

Yuki : During that season I think Kyoto City tried to disperse tourists to other spots so that popular areas didn’t become too concentrated with people.

Hiro : That sounds like it would have been an effective idea. Kyoto has many hidden beauty spots, so it would be better if people could get information about them and visit those places too.

Yuki : Yeah, for sure. (212 words)

■ Summary 29 DL

次の英文は、上記の会話を要約したものです。音声を聞いて、(　　) を埋めましょう。

When Hiro explains that he was (1.   ) late for school, Yuki recalls the tough time she had in her first year of college. Since overtourism (2.   ) the (3.   ) system in Kyoto at that time, she sometimes (4.   ) her bus and was almost late for school. Yuki also explains the measures that Kyoto City took against (5.   ) during that period.

Reading

次の英文を読んで、後の問いに答えましょう。

Kyoto Tackles "Overtourism"

"Overtourism" is when **excessive** tourists cause a variety of problems for a city or country. The term originated in 2016 on a website about tourism, and has become an **essential** concept in **both** business **and** academic conversations about tourism.

Too many tourists can **lead to** road **congestion**, **traffic jams**, and **noise pollution**. This may **inconvenience** local people and **undermine** the appeal of **tourist attractions**.

Before the **coronavirus pandemic**, Japan's goal had been to increase the number of **inbound** visitors to 40 million by 2020. However, due to its appeal among tourists, Kyoto started experiencing overtourism several years before that goal was reached. At its busiest, 50 million tourists a year used to visit the city before the pandemic started. Near the **World Heritage Site** Kiyomizu Temple, it was common to see long lines of people waiting for buses. The locals **were used to** these scenes, but were especially troubled by the heavier traffic in the fall when people wanted to view the fall leaves. There was also **noise pollution** from the increased number of private lodgings, called *minpaku*.

Kyoto tried to tackle the overtourism problems by dispersing people based on different times, areas, and seasons. For example, they promoted morning sightseeing at Nijo Castle to vary the times that people visited. Fushimi Ward used area dispersion by planning tours that focused on attracting visitors to places other than Fushimi Inari Taisha, such as **sake breweries**. For seasonal dispersion, the city tried to attract tourists in the early summer **off-season**. According to one expert, Kyoto City's efforts could be a case study for other tourist cities worldwide.

(266 words)

Notes

excessive 過剰な / essential 重要な / both A and B A と B 両方で / lead to ～（という結果）につながる / congestion 混雑 / traffic jam 交通渋滞 / noise pollution 騒音公害 / inconvenience 迷惑をかける / undermine いつの間にか害する / tourist attraction 観光名所 / coronavirus pandemic コロナウイルス感染症の大流行 / inbound 本国行きの / World Heritage Site 世界遺産 / be used to ～に慣れている / noise pollution 騒音公害 / sake brewery 酒蔵 / off-season 閑散期の

Comprehension I

本文から読み取れる内容を、フローチャートに日本語で記入しましょう。

1st paragraph

・Overtourism は (1.   ) によって引き起こされる問題。

・(2.   ) 年に、ある観光情報サイトで生まれた。

・観光ビジネスや学術的な話題の両方で (3.   ) 概念になる。

2nd paragraph

・観光地にあまりの多くの観光客

⇒ 道路の (4.   )、(5.   ) や騒音等の様々な問題に。

⇒ (6.   ) にとって迷惑 ／ 観光地の魅力を損なう。

3rd paragraph

・2020 年までの日本の目標：(7.   ) 外国人旅行者数を 4,000 万人に。

・年間 (8.   ) 万人以上の観光客が訪れる (9.   ) で overtourism。

(10.   ) の清水寺の近くの大通りのバス待ちの長蛇の列

民泊による (11.   )

4th paragraph

・京都の (12.   ) ・場所・時期の分散化

時間：二条城での朝観光　　場所：伏見区の (13.   ) ツーリズム

時期：(14.   ) の初夏に誘致

Comprehension 2

本文の内容について、以下の質問に答えましょう。

1. Which statement is true about overtourism?

   a. It can be a factor that ruins a great tourist attraction.
   b. The term was created on a business information website.
   c. It is an essential concept in discussions about historical sites.
   d. Tokyo is already experiencing problems caused by overtourism.

2. Which statement is true about Kyoto?

   a. Kyoto has been suffering from overtourism for decades.
   b. Kyoto attracts more than 15 million tourists a year.
   c. It is a major tourist city attracting tourists from overseas.
   d. People waiting in line for the bus is an unusual sight for local residents.

Writing

日本語に合うように、単語を並び替えて文章を完成させましょう。文頭にくる語も小文字にしてあります。

1. 今朝、電車に乗り遅れるところだった。
   (my / missed / I / train / almost) this morning.

   ____.

2. 彼女は聡明でもあり、思いやり深くもある。
   (and / is / compassionate / she / both / intelligent).

   ____.

3. 風邪は万病のもと。
   A cold (all / to / illnesses / kinds / often / of / leads).

   ____.

Expressions for Problem Solving

・Let me explain …　（～を説明させてください）

Let me explain the details of this graph.

・I doubt if …　（～かどうかは疑問です）

I doubt if the data will give us a solution to the problem.

・Everyone knows that …　（誰でも～と知っています）

Everyone knows that it is the most practical way.

Extension Activity

Group Work

インバウンド旅行による観光公害への対策案をグループで話し合い、メモしましょう。

Notes

Writing

グループで出し合った案の中からいいと思ったものを３つ選んで書き出しましょう。

日本語

1. ______________________________
2. ______________________________
3. ______________________________

英語

1. ______________________________
2. ______________________________
3. ______________________________

Speaking

３つの案をグループ内で発表し合いましょう。Evaluation Form にお互いの評価を記入しましょう。

Unit 12

Esports

eスポーツの人気を高めるには？

Warm up

日本語の意味を表す英語を選択肢から選んで（　　）に記号を記入しましょう。

eスポーツ
Esports

1. に参加する（　　）
2. 法的問題（　　）
3. 流れる（　　）
4. 賞金（　　）
5. 競争的な（　　）
6. 競技会（　　）
7. ～ほど…ではない（　　）
8. 先日（　　）
9. と違った（　　）
10. テレビゲーム（　　）

a. video game	b. competition	c. not as … as ～	d. prize money
e. legal issue	f. the other day	g. participate in	h. stream
i. unlike	j. competitive		

Dialogue 31 DL

次の会話を聞きましょう。その後ペアで会話を音読しましょう。

Taka : Have you heard of esports?

Miku : Yeah, I have. They're competitive events using video games, right?

Taka: Right. The other day, there was a big esports competition to determine the number one esports player among university students in Japan. It was streamed live on YouTube. Did you see it?

Miku: No, I didn't know about it. Are esports that popular?

Taka: Yeah. There's also a tournament for Japanese high school students, and some people want to make it an official event at the Olympics. But they're not as popular in Japan as overseas.

Miku: Oh really? Why?

Taka: First of all, the prize money is different. The prize money for some esports tournaments overseas is as much as ¥3 billion, but in Japan, I think ¥100 million is the highest cash prize. I heard some legal issues prevent the prize money from being higher.

Miku: And I guess not many people know about esports here yet.

Taka: I think that's a part of it. Plus many people don't know that playing esports can be profitable for players.

Miku: Well, it's nice that people of all ages can participate in the tournaments. I heard that unlike physical sports, esports players can continue playing even after they turn 70. That's nice, isn't it?

(202 words)

Summary

次の英文は、上記の会話を要約したものです。音声を聞いて、(　　) を埋めましょう。

Taka and Miku are talking about esports, (1. 　　　　　　) sports that use (2. 　　　　　　). There are esports (3. 　　　　　　) for college and high school students in Japan, but esports are (4a. 　　　　　　) popular in Japan (4b. 　　　　　　) overseas. One of the reasons for this is the difference in the amount of (5. 　　　　　　). Another reason is that esports are not well known and many people do not know that playing esports can be profitable for players.

Reading 33 DL

次の英文を読んで、後の問いに答えましょう。

Japan to Set Ambitious Target for Esports Expansion Through 2025

The global esports market is **currently** said to be worth ¥100 billion. It is expanding rapidly in the U.S., China, and parts of Europe. **On the other hand**, there is little recognition of competitive gaming as a sport in Japan. In order to **catch up with** the global trend, the Japanese government is trying to expand the esports industry, **with the aim of** stimulating local economies and promoting social participation among **people with disabilities**.

Attempts at the local level to use esports for health and social purposes have already begun. For example, a **non-profit organization** in Saitama City has been created to set up local esports events for **retired residents**. The goals of the events are to maintain the health of the participants and improve their **cognitive functions**.

In addition, to promote social participation, Takasaki City in Gunma Prefecture held an esports event for people with disabilities for the first time in Japan. The company that organized the event also provides employment support aimed at expanding the possibilities of people with disabilities.

The **Ministry of Economy, Trade and Industry (METI) estimated** that the economic effect on the economy by esports will reach at least ¥285 billion over the next several years. According to one marketing research firm, the size of the Japanese esports market is expected to grow from ¥6.1 billion to ¥15.3 billion in only a few years' time. (230 words)

Notes

currently 現在は / on the other hand これに反して / catch up with ～に追いつく / with the aim of ～を目的として / people with disabilities 障がい者 / attempt 試み / non-profit organization 非営利組織 / retired resident 退職した地元住民 / cognitive function 認知機能 / Ministry of Economy, Trade and Industry 経済産業省 / estimate 試算する

Comprehension 1

本文から読み取れる内容を、フローチャートに日本語で記入しましょう。

Unit 12

1st paragraph

・世界のｅスポーツ市場は (1.　　　　　　　) 円の規模だと言われている。

・(2.　　　　　　　)、日本でのスポーツ競技としての認知度は低い。

・日本政府は世界の潮流に (3.　　　　　　　) → ｅスポーツ市場の拡大へ

(4.　　　　　　　) の活性化や (5.　　　　　　　) の社会参加促進を目的に。

2nd paragraph

・地域社会の活性化の例：さいたま市の (6.　　　　　　　) 開催のイベント

(7.　　　　　　　) を対象

・目的は (8.　　　　　　　) の向上と高齢者の健康維持。

3rd paragraph

・(9.　　　　　　　) の社会参加促進の例：群馬県高崎市でのイベント

障がい者を対象－日本初　就労支援も実施する会社による。

4th paragraph

・(10.　　　　　　　) 省の試算：地域経済への経済効果少なくとも 2,850 億円

あるマーケティングリサーチ会社の予測：

市場規模　2019 年 (11.　　　　　　　) 円から → 2023 年 (12.　　　　　　　) 円に

Comprehension 2

本文の内容について、以下の質問に答えましょう。

1. Which statement is true about the Japanese esports industry?

a. Esports have a high level of recognition in Japan.

b. Esports events can lead to development in local areas.

c. The esports market in Japan is said to be worth ¥100 billion.

d. The esports market in Japan is expanding as rapidly as it is in Europe.

2. Which is the best alternative title for the reading passage?

a. Why Are Esports So Unpopular in Japan?

b. How to Become a Japanese Esports Player

c. The Future of the Esports Industry in Japan

d. Ministry of Economy, Trade and Industry's Policies on Esports

Writing

日本語に合うように、単語を並び替えて文章を完成させましょう。文頭にくる語も小文字にしてあります。

1. それははたから見るほど容易ではない。

It's (as / looks / not / it / easy / as).

____.

2. 他方で、経験から学ぶ人もいます。

(hand / on / the / other), some people learn from experience.

____.

3. 海外留学をする目的で英語を勉強し始めた。

I started studying (aim / studying / the / abroad / of / with / English).

____.

Expressions for Problem Solving

・I see what you mean, but … （言いたいことはわかりますが～）

I see what you mean, but I think it's too expensive.

・As far as I can see, … （私が知る限り、～）

As far as I can see, we need more drastic measures to deal with the declining birthrate.

・What is your opinion about …? （～についてあなたの意見は？）

What is your opinion about the current agenda?

Extension Activity

Group Work

e スポーツの人気を高めるための具体案をグループで出し合い、メモしましょう。

Notes

Writing

グループで出し合った案の中からいいと思ったものを３つ選んで書き出しましょう。

日本語

1. ____________________
2. ____________________
3. ____________________

英語

1. ____________________
2. ____________________
3. ____________________

Speaking

３つの案をグループ内で発表し合いましょう。Evaluation Form にお互いの評価を記入しましょう。

Unit 13

Sleep Deprivation

睡眠不足は寝だめで解消！？

Warm up

日本語の意味を表す英語を選択肢から選んで（　　）に記号を記入しましょう。

睡眠不足

Sleep Deprivation

1. 目覚まし時計をセットする（　　）
2. 専門家（　　）
3. 治る（　　）
4. 昼寝する（　　）
5. ～を取り戻す（　　）
6. 用語・言い回し（　　）
7. 睡眠障害（　　）
8. 不足（　　）
9. 睡眠負債（　　）
10. 蓄積する（　　）

a. catch up on	**b.** accumulate	**c.** deficiency	**d.** expert
e. get over	**f.** sleep debt	**g.** sleep disorder	**h.** term
i. take a nap	**j.** set an alarm		

Dialogue 34 DL

次の会話を聞きましょう。その後ペアで会話を音読しましょう。

Toshi : I' m so happy it' s Friday!

Penny: Do you have any exciting plans this weekend?

Toshi : No, I’m just going to catch up on my sleep. I haven’t had enough sleep recently because of all the tests and assignments.

Penny: Have you heard the term “sleep debt”?

Toshi : No, I haven’t. What does it mean?

Penny: Sleep debt is the result of not getting enough sleep for a long period of time. You probably think that you can make up for your lost sleep on the weekend, right? But if you sleep too long on the weekend, it’s difficult for you to go to sleep on Sunday night. So the deficiency continues the following week, and your lack of sleep continues to accumulate.

Toshi : That’s me exactly! How can I get out of this cycle? Is there any way to make up for lost sleep?

Penny: Well, what you should do is try to get up at the same time every morning.

Toshi : That sounds doable. I just need to set an alarm. Do you have other suggestions?

Penny: Uh, maybe you can take a nap early in the afternoon. But don’t sleep too long.

Toshi : OK. That’s easy too. You’re like a sleep expert!

Penny: Actually, I had a sleep disorder, but I’m getting over it now.

(206 words)

■ Summary

次の英文は、上記の会話を要約したものです。音声を聞いて、(　　)を埋めましょう。

Toshi needs to (1.   ) his sleep because he has not been sleeping enough lately. Penny thinks he might have (2.   ), which is the result of sleep (3.   ) that (4.   ) over a period of time. Penny says one thing he can do to help is to get up at the same time every morning. Penny also suggests that he can (5.   ) in the early afternoon.

Reading 36 DL

次の英文を読んで、後の問いに答えましょう。

Will Power Nap Project Help the Sleep-Deprived?

Studies have shown that people in Japan are little aware of the importance of sleep, thus many people become sleep deprived and have trouble doing their work **properly**. To improve this situation and raise public awareness about sleep, the "Power Nap Project" was formed.

A power nap is a short sleep **lasting** 15 to 20 minutes. It is intended to clear your mind and **revitalize** you so that you can focus on your work later. The Power Nap Project has already been introduced by some companies.

One of the goals of the project is for organizations to create a suitable environment for napping. For example, some participating companies are now offering **hoodie blankets** to workers. This is done to promote the concept that employees can take a nap while they are at work. Employees are also encouraged to talk with each other, and some of the companies have their employees wake each other up **in turns**.

Many workers involved in the Power Nap Project say that they feel refreshed and that their workplace communication has increased, which has led to improved teamwork.

It is expected that in the near future, naps will be required to be included in the work schedules of Japanese companies. This will **benefit** both the companies and their employees. The project has already begun, so let's just wait and see if napping becomes a natural part of company life.

(233 words)

Notes

properly 適切に / last 続く / revitalize 活性化する / hoodie blanket フード付きの毛布 / in turns 交替で / benefit 利益になる

Comprehension 1

本文から読み取れる内容を、フローチャートに日本語で記入しましょう。

1st & 2nd paragraphs

・日本では睡眠に関する (1.　　　　) が低い

⇒ (2.　　　　　　　　) になり、適切に仕事ができなくなる

・Power Nap

⇒ (3.　　　　　　　　) 分間の睡眠で、スッキリして業務に (4.　　　　　　) できる

⇒ Power Nap Project が (5.　　　　　　) に導入されつつある

3rd & 4th paragraphs

・昼寝をしやすい環境づくり　例：(6.　　　　　　　　　　　) の提供

・従業員同士が交替で (7.　　　　　　　　　　) 会社もある

・昼寝が気分転換となり、(8.　　　　　　　　　　) が増え、(9.　　　　　　　　) の改善につながる

5th paragraph

・近い将来、日本企業では (10.　　　　　　　　　　　　　　) が必須となる

・昼寝は (11.　　　　　　　　) と (12.　　　　　　　　) の双方にとって有益である

Comprehension 2

本文の内容について、以下の質問に答えましょう。

1. What is power napping?
   - a. Distributing hoodie blankets to all employees
   - b. Encouraging employees to sleep long hours
   - c. Sleeping enough hours so that one feels refreshed
   - d. Taking naps for a short period of time

2. Which is NOT a benefit of power naps in the workplace?
   - a. Employees communicate with each other more often.
   - b. It helps people work more effectively in the office.
   - c. Many people become more loyal to their company.
   - d. Workers can concentrate on their job after a nap.

Writing

日本語に合うように、単語を並び替えて文章を完成させましょう。文頭にくる語も小文字にしてあります。

1. 眠いときに、仕事に集中できる方法はありますか？

   (any way / focus on / your duties / is / there / to) when you are sleepy?

   ____?

2. あなたにできることは、15分間昼寝をすることですね。

   (take a nap / do / can / is / what / you) for 15 minutes.

   ____.

3. ほとんどの従業員は職場でのコミュニケーションの大切さについて意識しています。

   Most employees (aware of / workplace communication / the importance / are / of).

   ____.

Expressions for Problem Solving

- Is there any way to …? （～する方法はありますか？）

  Is there any way to catch up on my sleep?

- What you can do is … （あなたにできることは～です）

  What you can do is go to bed early.

- Do you have other suggestions? （他に提案はありますか？）

  All of the ideas sound good. **Do you have other suggestions?**

Extension Activity

Group Work

睡眠負債に陥らない対策法や良質の睡眠をとれる方法をグループで出し合い、メモしましょう。

Notes

Writing

グループで出し合った案の中からいいと思ったものを３つ選んで書き出しましょう。

日本語
1. ______
2. ______
3. ______

英語
1. ______
2. ______
3. ______

Speaking

３つの案をグループ内で発表し合いましょう。Evaluation Form にお互いの評価を記入しましょう。

Unit 14

AI

人工知能と共存できるか？

Warm up

日本語の意味を表す英語を選択肢から選んで（　　）に記号を記入しましょう。

AI
人工知能と共存できるか？

1. すべてができるとは限らない（　　）
2. 取って代わる（　　）
3. 課題（　　）
4. 最近（　　）
5. 超える（　　）
6. ～と共存する（　　）
7. 翻訳する（　　）
8. 認識する（　　）
9. 進歩（　　）
10. 特徴（　　）

a. lately	**b.** surpass	**c.** progress	**d.** translate
e. recognize	**f.** feature	**g.** replace	**h.** cannot do everything
i. challenge	**j.** coexist with		

Dialogue 37 DL

次の会話を聞きましょう。その後ペアで会話を音読しましょう。

Sandy : I've been hearing a lot about AI lately.

Mike : Yeah, I saw on the news that AI technology has surpassed the ability of professional chess, *go*, and *shogi* players.

Sandy : With all the progress in AI development, AI can now do many things. For example, it can translate languages, drive cars, recognize images, and so on.

Mike : Also, AI can give you directions or search for a restaurant when you use some smartphone functions.

Sandy : They are very useful features. But I've heard that there is a high possibility that AI will replace many jobs in the future.

Mike : If that happens, will there be any jobs left for humans to do?

Sandy : I think so. I don't believe AI can do everything.

Mike : Yes, that's true. I think there are some jobs that humans will always do better than AI, such as care work.

Sandy : Exactly. I think the challenge for the future will be how well humans can coexist with AI. To live with AI, we need to have a good command of how to use it properly.

Mike : Yeah, and after all, AI is created by humans. (181 words)

Summary 38 DL

次の英文は、上記の会話を要約したものです。音声を聞いて、(　　) を埋めましょう。

Sandy and Mike are talking about the progress of AI technology. AI technology has (1. 　　　　　　) human skill in playing some games like chess and *shogi*. AI can also do many things like (2. 　　　　　　　　), driving, and recognizing images. However, Sandy is worried that AI will (3. 　　　　　　) humans in the workforce in the future, but she also believes that AI (4. 　　　　　　　　　　　). Mike agrees and thinks there are some jobs humans will always do better than AI. They think that the challenge for the future will be how well we can (5. 　　　　　　　　　　) AI.

Reading 39 DL

次の英文を読んで、後の問いに答えましょう。

Artificial Intelligence Making Sushi for Japanese Chain Store

Kura Sushi is a popular **conveyer belt sushi chain** store in Japan. They are currently offering a unique chance to try **aged** fish sushi made with the help of artificial intelligence (AI).

The aging of fish is done because the process makes the meat tastier. However, it is difficult to do and requires someone with special training and knowledge. Therefore, it is usually only found at **traditional** sushi shops, not regular conveyor belt chain stores. But Kura Sushi has changed this by placing cloth wrapped fish in an **AI-controlled** environment to successfully age fish.

Thanks to this technology, Kura Sushi is able to **mass-produce** aged fish and offer it on its *nigiri* sushi menu. Currently, the process of aging fish by AI has successfully been completed for its tuna and **yellowtail** *nigiri* sushi.

Kura Sushi has not stopped at using AI to just age fish. It has also begun using a special **app** called "Tuna Scope." Tuna Scope was developed by the advertising company Dentsu, and it **identifies** the best parts of a tuna to use for making sushi. Tuna Scope does this by using AI technology to analyze a **cross-section** of the tail. Thus, Kura Sushi can **ensure** that its customers get the freshest and most high-quality fish possible.

(210 words)

Notes

conveyer belt sushi chain 回転寿司チェーン店 / aged 熟成した / traditional 従来の / AI-controlled AIで制御された / mass-produce 大量生産する / yellowtail ブリ / app アプリ / identify 特定する / cross-section 断面 / ensure 確実にする

Comprehension 1

本文から読み取れる内容を、フローチャートに日本語で記入しましょう。

1st paragraph

・日本の回転寿司チェーンのくら寿司は、人工知能を用いて (1.　　　　　　　　) を使った寿司をメニューに加えようとしている。

2nd paragraph

・魚を熟成させるためには、熟成過程および熟練の寿司職人を必要とするため、回転寿司チェーンよりも (2.　　　　　　　　) でよく見かける。

・魚肉を (3.　　　　　　) で包んで (4.　　　　　　　　) に置いておくことで、魚の (5.　　　　　　) に成功した。

3rd paragraph

・AIのおかげで、くら寿司は握り寿司用に熟成魚を (6.　　　　　　) できるようになった。特に (7.　　　　　　) と (8.　　　　　　) において、熟成プロセスを完成させつつある。

4th paragraph

・(9.　　　　　　) による生のマグロの熟成に加えて、くら寿司は電通が開発した “Tuna Scope” という (10.　　　　　　) を使用した。これは人工知能を使って尾の (11.　　　　　　) を分析することで、マグロの最適な部位を特定する。これにより、店は (12.　　　　　　) に新鮮で高品質な魚を提供できる。

Comprehension 2

本文の内容について、以下の質問に答えましょう。

1. How do Kura Sushi age their fish?
   a. Wrap the fish in a cloth and leave it to sit in an uncontrolled environment
   b. Wrap the fish in a cloth and put it in a refrigerator for a short time
   c. Put uncovered fish in a place where the temperature is monitored by specially trained staff
   d. Put cloth wrapped fish in a place where humidity and temperature are controlled by AI

2. What kind of company developed the app “Tuna Scope”?

a. A Japanese sushi restaurant chain
b. A Japanese advertising agency
c. A Japanese fish company
d. A Japanese conveyer belt company

Writing

日本語に合うように、単語を並び替えて文章を完成させましょう。文頭にくる語も小文字にしてあります。

1. トムのすばやい対応のおかげで、私たちは何とか課題を仕上げることができた。
(to / Tom’s / support / quick / thanks), we managed to finish our assignment.

____.

2. すべての魚が海に住んでいるわけではない。
(fish / lives / every / not) in the sea.

____.

3. 私はあなたがそのような愚かなことをしていないと思う。
I (you / don’t / that / believe / did / silly / such a) thing.

____.

Expressions for Problem Solving

・not every … （全てが～とは限らない）

Not everybody agreed with Judy’s opinion.

・Thanks to … （～のおかげで）

Thanks to the weather, we enjoyed our camping trip.

・I don’t believe that …（私は～ではないと思う）

I don’t believe that they will win the game.

Extension Activity

Group Work

人工知能と人間がいかに共存していくべきか、その対策案をグループで出し合い、メモしましょう。

Notes

Writing

グループで出し合った案の中からいいと思ったものを３つ選んで書き出しましょう。

日本語

1. ______________________________
2. ______________________________
3. ______________________________

英語

1. ______________________________
2. ______________________________
3. ______________________________

Speaking

３つの案をグループ内で発表し合いましょう。Evaluation Form にお互いの評価を記入しましょう。

Unit 15 Column 3

Problem Solving Beyond the Classroom

Problem solving is a part of daily life. We do it every day without realizing it. In fact, your day may even start with problem solving. Think about the times you have overslept causing you to run late for university or a part-time job. How did you solve that problem? However, more advanced problem-solving skills are required to **tackle** larger, more complex issues. Indeed, good problem solving is a very **desirable** skill to employers. Being able to **identify** a problem (or **potential** problem), its cause, and finding an appropriate solution can lead to important changes and improvements. Japan has many famous examples of creative and effective solutions to problems. Here are some examples:

- Japan is famous for its building technology to help decrease the risks that earthquakes cause.
- Toyota developed the Prius to **address** the need for more environmentally friendly vehicles.
- Emojis were created to help communicate information quickly and effectively on early cellphones.

Of course, not all solutions to problems need to be world-changing, but developing your problem-solving skills will **definitely** benefit you inside and outside of the classroom.

Notes

tackle 取り組む / desirable 望ましい / identify 確認する、見定める / potential 潜在的な / address 対応する / definitely 絶対に

Comprehension

本文から読み取れる内容を、フローチャートに日本語で記入しましょう。

1st paragraph

日常的な問題解決の例：

寝過ごして大学やアルバイトに（1.　　　　　）とき

日本の創造的かつ効果的な問題解決の例：

・（2.　　　　　）が引き起こすリスクを減らすための（3.　　　　　）

・（4.　　　　　）車のニーズに応えるためのプリウス開発

・初期の（5.　　　　　）で素早く効果的に情報を伝えるための（6.　　　　　）

2nd paragraph

優れた（7.　　　　　）は雇用者からも求められており、教室の中でも外でも必ず（8.　　　　　）。

Think about Column 3, "Problem Solving Beyond the Classroom." Can you think of other famous solutions to problems not mentioned in this textbook? Briefly explain the problems and the solutions.

Problems

Solutions

Word Search (Units 11-14)

Find the words in the puzzle. Words can go in any direction.
Words can share a letter as they cross over each other.

E	D	H	V	V	Z	M	Z	N	S	Y	R	M	T	N
S	E	B	O	C	J	V	D	H	O	E	E	N	O	H
R	F	T	W	S	L	S	M	D	V	I	F	I	J	Y
E	I	E	B	F	C	L	F	I	Y	K	T	R	B	U
P	C	C	R	L	W	M	T	D	J	S	V	C	S	W
S	I	W	S	K	Q	A	M	U	E	L	P	R	E	A
I	E	R	F	V	L	Z	A	G	D	K	N	S	A	S
D	N	Q	A	I	W	T	N	A	N	G	M	X	L	C
B	C	W	Z	C	G	O	U	L	T	E	X	Y	N	F
R	Y	E	L	G	C	I	F	Z	I	T	I	F	A	E
T	E	W	I	Q	Z	Y	F	F	I	B	E	P	R	B
S	T	R	E	A	M	W	H	N	X	E	V	M	A	I
C	T	X	F	H	H	O	C	S	L	F	H	G	P	Y
S	S	A	P	R	U	S	B	F	A	S	X	V	U	T
F	T	M	F	T	K	J	H	K	L	R	C	E	E	X

Words

attempt / congestion / deficiency / disperse / revitalize /
section / stream / surpass

参考文献

【Unit 01】

https://www.bbc.co.uk/programmes/p06ccx9v 参照

https://www.who.int/china/news/detail/28-03-2018-are-our-smart-phones-affecting-our-mental-health- *News release　China*, March 28, 2018 参照

【Unit 03】

Updated WHO advice for international traffic in relation to the outbreak of the novel coronavirus 2019-nCoV 参照

【Unit 04】

www.udon-soujyu.co.jp/suberanudon/suberanudon.html 参照

写真提供：うどん双樹　文章：うどん双樹ホームページより著者訳

【Unit 06】

https://www.st-andrews.ac.uk/students/advice/leaflets/stress/ 参照

【Unit 07】

https://japantoday.com/category/national/students-complain-of-being-exploited-in-part-time-jobs-survey-shows *Japan Today*, Nov. 10, 2015 参照

【Unit 08】

https://japantoday.com/category/features/kuchikomi/what-to-do-about-elderly-drivers *Japan Today*, Nov. 26, 2016 参照

【Unit 09】

https://gooddo.jp/magazine/oceans/marine_pollution/plastic_garbage/ gooddo マガジン参照

【Unit 11】

https://www3.nhk.or.jp/nhkworld/en/news/backstories/264/ *NHK World*, Oct. 11, 2018 参照

【Unit 12】

https://www.japantimes.co.jp/news/2020/03/29/national/japan-expansion-esports-economy-2025/ *Kyodo News*, Mar. 28, 2020 及び https://www.atpress.ne.jp/news/187984 参照

【Unit 13】

https://japantoday.com/category/features/lifestyle/with-sleep-deprivation-a-growing-problem-in-japan-companies-introduce-power-nap-project *Japan Today*, Feb. 9, 2020 参照

【Unit 14】

https://japantoday.com/category/features/food/japanese-conveyor-belt-sushi-restaurant-chain-makes-sushi-with-help-of-artificial-intelligence *Japan Today*, Nov. 30, 2020 参照

Let's Find a Solution!

PBL（問題解決型学習）ではじめる総合英語 ―学習者から探究者へ―

1　刷　2023 年 1 月 15 日　[B-946]

著　者　赤尾　美和　Miwa Akao
西垣　佐理　Sari Nishigaki
幸重　美津子　Mitsuko Yukishige
工藤　多恵　Tae Kudo
松田　紀子　Noriko Matsuda
板垣　静香　Shizuka Itagaki
ジョリー キム　Kym Jolley
英文校閲　ジョリー キム　Kym Jolley

発行者　南雲　一範　Kazunori Nagumo
発行所　株式会社　南雲堂
〒162-0801　東京都新宿区山吹町 361
NAN'UN-DO CO.,Ltd.
361 Yamabuki-cho, Shinjuku-ku, Tokyo 162-0801, Japan
振替口座：00160-0-46863
TEL：03-3268-2311(営業部：学校関係)
TEL：03-3268-2384(営業部：書店関係)
TEL：03-3268-2387(編集部)
FAX：03-3269-2486

編集者　加藤　敦

組　版　中西　史子

装　丁　N スタジオ

検　印　省略

コード　ISBN 978-4-523-17946-7　C0082

Printed in Japan

E-mail　nanundo@post.email.ne.jp
URL　https://www.nanun-do.co.jp